Let The Good Rhymes Roll

Volume Two

Best wishes,

Peter

Peter Gibbs

ISBN: 9798844152863

For Sally, Grandmére, Peg and Jeanie Baby.

With grateful thanks to Vivvie and Marc.

CONTENTS

FOREWORD

Welcome to the second volume of
my anthology of poetry.

These verses again cover a multitude of themes,
not least the scourge of the worldwide
pandemic and Russia's brutal invasion
of Ukraine.

As well as these dramas, they have been
inspired by romance, travel, the beauty of
nature, emotions, humour and significant
events in my life and those of others.

Many feature the North Somerset seaside town
of Clevedon – beloved by generations of poets
and where I have lived since 1968.

I hope you enjoy reading these poems as much
as I have enjoyed writing them.

ALL BOARD THE CLEVEDON RAILWAY

All aboard the Clevedon Railway
Come along and take a ride
Miniature, the track and engine
Sit on coaches, not inside
Journey's start by bouncy castle
Old town station here revived
Whistle toot signals departure
With passengers who've just arrived
Round Salthouse Fields with rails encircled
Past the lake and tennis play
Happy children, beaming adults
Here to share their seaside day.

WOODLAND SNOWDROPS

Snowdrops in the Dial Hill woods
That rarely see the snow
Hinting at the coming Spring
The season's preview show
Perfect petalled whiteness
On slender stems of green
Lighting up the woodland floor
With luminescent sheen
All too soon they fade from sight
When they have had their day
Making way for bright crocus
And daffodils asway.

ATISHOO – A MERRY CHRISTMAS?

To those at home with COVID
Who have to isolate
I send these festive greetings
To help you celebrate
The trip that you were making
Your plans for Christmas Day
Now thanks to flow test positive
Are all in disarray
You haven't got a turkey
Nor even a plum pud
It's hard to feel all happy
Even if you should
Like the Queen at Windsor
You're not where you would be
Joining hands with relatives
And singing merrily
But even though it's difficult
Just find a little cheer
It won't be long before you're told
That you are now All Clear.

NUT SO CLEVER

Oh, pretty paddle boarder
Please spare a thought for me
While you're there on the water
And I'm here up a tree
Through all the lengthy summer days
I've searched the woodland floor
And lofty, bendy branches
To gather winter's store

But though I may be nimble
My fingers are so small
I sometimes go and drop my nuts
And sadly watch them fall
Into the flowing Avon
Where you have come for sport
It would have been so helpful
If you a few had caught
I know I'm not so handsome
As others coloured red
But surely that should never mean
I starve while they're well fed
So next time you come paddling
Please bring along with you
A bag that's full to bursting
With walnuts and cashew.

HEART OF THE HIGH STREET

We've missed the shops and businesses
Who helped our town to tick
Forced to put up shutters
So we should not fall sick
They've always been our lifeblood
Served us throughout the days
From gifts to books and chocolates
And took a lot to faze
They might not sell necessities
They're wanted all the same
Now lockdown's eased they need us
And we will share the blame
If they don't have our custom
To get back on their feet
Without all these sole traders
No High Street is complete.

EASTER MARSHES

New calves born on windswept marshland
Fresh grass where they're settled down
Close by stand their so proud parents
With their offspring black and brown
Out atop a stony island
Avocets their courting make
Seeking there the perfect nest site
Amid the calls across the lake
Spoonbills busy sieving shallows
Oyster catchers join the throng
Little plover scurries madly
'Gainst the background of lark's song

Swallows here to barn returning
Summer's promise on the wing
Black lambs in a field just gambolling
Breathing in the joy of Spring
In the reeds the nesting mute swans
Underneath a cloudless sky
Easter Sunday at Steart Marshes
As the sunlit hours flow by.

HUDDERSFIELD CANAL WALK - for Nige

Ghost mills that once wove cotton
Disused like mills of wool
The high Pennines dividing
Where industry did rule
The rushing Colne alongside
Canal in stone banks tamed
Past monumental building
For lost Titanic named
Long gone the busy workers
Who once world record made
Fleece to wearer in two hours
A fine suit then displayed.
From Huddersfield to Marsden
Where mournful church bells rang
When Luddites fighting progress
Were taken out to hang
Beyond, the Standedge Tunnel
The longest and most high
And deepest in the country
But closed, so we passed by.

SUNSET SILHOUETTES

Silhouettes in the sunset
The old pier standing proud
Figures on the slipway
'Neath orange bands of cloud
Far across the water
The sun has dipped from sight
Its rays now swiftly fading
As quietly comes the night
The silver sea now burnished
With just a tinge of gold
As darkness lays its mantle
To seaside town enfold.

GORDANO LANDSCAPE

Walton Church in peaceful valley
Cottage cluster here surround
A perfect sight to greet the morn
With green fields spreading all around
The golf course waiting players
As fairways are close mown
A hillside sloping downwards
With wild flowers gaily sown
Woodland to horizon
Far highway cutting through
The landscape of Gordano
As day begins anew.

SAILING THE SEVERN SEA

From out the Severn estuary
Towards the open sea
The countless ships went sailing
Towards their history
Cabot heading boldly
To find his Newfoundland
Led the way for others
As 'cross the globe they spanned
Pirates lusting treasure
Upon the Spanish Main
Merchants seeking commerce
Their profits to maintain
Fish to feed the Catholics
Exchanged for finest wine
Sugar and tobacco
Produced through slavers' crime
Where Vikings once sailed longships
Vast vessels with their loads
Cross this liquid canvas
With cars to clog our roads
Twice daily sure as clockwork
Immense tides rise and fall
A mighty force of nature
That will survive us all.

PENICILLIN PLAQUE

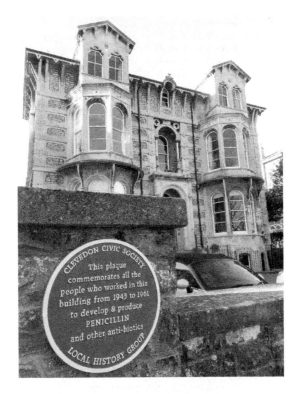

On Elton Road in Clevedon
And grand walls there within
Would busy wartime workers
Create penicillin
Unnoticed and unlauded
They followed Fleming's lead
Where he had grown mould slowly
They made it here with speed
So forces who were wounded
Would see another day
Improving their survival with
Infections kept at bay
Those to whom they owed their lives
Were ones they never met
But there's a plaque upon a wall
So we will not forget.

BENEATH CLEVEDON'S WAVES

In the sea before us
There's much we do not see
Beneath the waves a world that brims
With life's infinity
The noisy gulls cry overhead
While in the depths below
Creatures move at their own pace
The rapid and the slow
Cod with plaice and conger eel
There's even found catshark
Swimming oh so silently
Unseen here in the dark
Eels that seek Sargasso Sea
And there a place to breed
Pass by us on their journey
Fulfilling nature's need
Rivers and streams are here combined
In Severn Estuary
Muddy gravel beds sustain
Marine biology
Worms and crabs find nutrients
In turn they are the food
For all the busy waders
That in rock pools intrude
While out across the Channel
You may just catch a sight
As porpoise, seal and dolphin
Swim free as is their right.

BIRDY BOARDWALK

With feet all curled and twisted
This bird was in a mess
Hoping to get flying
Yet left in deep distress
All cosy in his Mummy's nest
But hopeless on the ground
His walking was a nightmare
Solution must be found
While some were just cold-hearted
His sorry plight ignored
One kind soul was moved to help
And make him shoes of board
So while it's still not easy
And hopping is quite hard
At least he has a fighting chance
Upon his soles of card.

DUNLIN AT DAWN

Low across the tide edge
Lit up by early sun
A darting flock of dunlin
Turn and wheel as one
Though starlings' murmurations
Paint sky with swirls of black
These pretty little waders
Shine white, as out and back
They fly from river inlet
Towards the Channel grey
Amid the lonely curlew call
Here seemingly at play.

SALLY'S CHERRY TREE

Like tulips yearly come to life
A beauteous tree recalls the wife
I handfast wed in Norfolk sun
With ribbons linked to join as one
As blossom smothers every bough
I recall the solemn vow
We made before the family gaze
Aware the limit of our days
Sadness softened through the years
Remembered laugh to chase the tears
Each cherry branch in memory
Of one who meant so much to me.

WINTER LAKE

Opal sky reflected
Across the lake of grey
Bare branch trees a backdrop
At dawn of winter day
Heavens slashed with orange
As students on a spree
Brave the icy water
Rather them than me.

NERO NOT HERO

Nero sat and fiddled
While outside his Rome burned
Trump did something similar
It seems he hadn't learned
That as his country's President
He had a solemn job
Not spending time a-Twittering
And whipping up a mob
For months before election
He spewed out countless lies
Said votes would just be stolen
So it was no surprise
That when he lost to Biden
He claimed it was a steal
And rallied his supporters
Who flocked to his appeal
To gather up in Washington
And march to where Congress
Were ratifying his defeat
And he met with success
But when the Capitol was stormed
The Chief was tucked away
Within his Office Oval
Throughout a shameful day
Democracy lay bleeding
But he would take no blame
Despite the wanton rampage
Conducted in his name
Not Great America regained
No matter what he pledged
He'd sown just deep division
And basest feelings dredged

When history now is written
No noble legacy
Just stain of two impeachments
Will live in memory.

CORRIDOR OF BLOSSOM

A corridor of blossom
Along a coastal way
An arch of virgin white above
A path along to stray
Blackthorn, gorse - fresh finery
As hedges spring to life
Bursting with vitality
While Man's locked down with strife
Splash of colours in the grass
Purple, violet, yellow
Flowers as a border
Ahead the route to follow.

WEIGHTY PROBLEM

I'm losing weight, I'm getting fat
Now who can see the sense in that
I'm gaining inches, losing pounds
My cheeks are jowls, I'm getting round
My waist goes out where it went in
And yet the scales say I am thin
Maybe it's all some devilish plot
That turns my tummy into pot.

DIAL HILL DAWNING

Dial Hill in the dawning
And not a soul abroad
Bird song through the woodland
Another memory stored
Light across the hillside
A track that leads to where
A seat and trig point overlook
Deserted cricket square
A view towards the Mendips
Softened in the haze
A warming breeze foretelling
The joy of summer days
Channel here stays hidden
Obscured behind the leaves
'Til down towards the waking town
The earthen path now weaves.

STEART MARSHES

A day at fine Steart Marshes
Not one to soon forget
With shelduck by the dozen
And breeding avocet
Swallows skimming meadows
Curlews, where the tide
Recedes revealing feeding grounds
The Channel here beside
Black-headed gulls a-plenty
Ringed plover bonus sight
A tick to please all birders
And who knows that you might
Come across a rarity
Just waiting to be seen
Above this precious wetland -
A water world of green.

COVID COURTESY

Today if you're out walking
It's common courtesy
To keep a social distance
If others you should see
On pavements that are narrow
Where traffic you can face
Step into the roadway
So walkers have their space
In shops the rule is simple
You have to wear a mask
And don't bunch up at check-outs
Staff shouldn't have to ask
When all are vaccinated
And Covid's in the past
The good manners we've adopted
Will hopefully still last.

LADYE BAY

A rocky, hidden inlet
Where children safely play
A Clevedon secret treasure
The lovely Ladye Bay
With water gently lapping
Upon the pebbly beach
Many steep steps leading down
The Channel shore to reach
White birds skimming westward
Across a pearly sea
Clear streams flowing downward
A babbling symphony
Sitting on a whitened trunk
From out a woodland torn
Looking down to Steep Holm
An hour beyond the dawn
The pier glimpsed round the headland
A path that leads ahead
Along the coast with views of Wales
To neighbouring Portishead.

WHAT A GAS

Image: Shutterstock.com

Cook, cook, cookability
That's the beauty of gas
But when I went and left it on
I felt a total ass
Our Katie's nose my saviour
When she picked up the scent
Of North Sea in my kitchen
She was just heaven-sent
The tale began the night before
With sausage-mash my dinner
When potatoes came to boil
The rings were changed to simmer
But faulty spark ignition
Had failed to light one flame
That knob was not turned fully
It's only me to blame
If there had been a mighty blast
At Old Park 101
And I had left this mortal coil
Blown to kingdom come.

JOHN'S BENCH – for Noelle

Within the sight of Clevedon
And overlooking lake
Where Noelle took to water
As John his ease would take
His birthplace bathed in sunshine
Newspaper in his hand
His family settled, happy
He knew that life was grand
His bench now marked forever
A plaque recording days
Looking 'cross the seafront
His town before his gaze.

NEVER IN OUR NAME

This is not Bristol fashion
Nor how we demonstrate
Filling streets with anger
Spewing out just hate
Police are there to make sure
We keep the rule of law
Without them there is anarchy
A taste of what we saw
Protection they afford us
The confidence they give
Secures our public safety
Without which we can't live
Those who besmirched our city
Should hang their heads in shame
Arson and destruction
Are never in our name
The parents of these rioters
And all to whom they're known
Should not condone with silence
But publicly disown.

ROWING IN HARMONY

Easing off the slipway
Into the rising tide
Trailers pulled to safety
As out the white boats ride
Oars at first held upright
Then dipped into the sea
Rowers making ready
Then linked in harmony
The pier here as the background
This Sunday in July
Exercise together
Beneath a summer sky.

GIFFORDS CIRCUS

We went to Giffords Circus
With all the usual crew
Before the big top opened
We headed up the queue
There is no show quite like it
With acts and music live
And kicking off the action
It's Tweedy and high five
Jugglers swift and acrobats
Tumbling here with practised ease
While far above the sawdust
A nimble girl on high trapeze

Horseback riders, doves a-winging
Slapstick fun and audience screams
Sequined costumes, showbiz glamour
Magic made of childhood dreams
All too soon the big finale
All too soon the parting bow
Next year they'll change the show completely
And we will never know just how.

SPRING'S SWEET PROMISE

Blossom on magnolia trees
Pastel pink and white
After months of greyness
A heart-uplifting sight
Daffodils in gardens
And lining sea view walks
Thrusting up from hidden bulbs
Blooms bright on sturdy stalks
Buds on bare branch bursting
Precursor here of leaves
A sign of Spring's sweet promise
For each one who believes
That Summer will return again
With chill replaced by heat
Longer days and warmer nights
A chance once more to meet
In pubs and parks and gardens
With family and friends
And hope that with the vaccines
This Covid nightmare ends.

HANDFAST WEDDING – for Sally

This is a different wedding
You said we never could
Be hitched, for then your pension
Would disappear for good
We haven't hired a vicar
No one has read the banns
But that has still not stopped us
From making nuptial plans
There'll not be any signatures
Before a registrar
And hopefully no shoes or cans
Or scribbling on our car
We won't be jetting far away
On foreign honeymoon
You bring me all my sunshine
Unlike that flaming June
With friends and family gathered
On this our special day
The timing is just perfect
For what I have to say

I love you, my own Sally
You've made my life complete
No doubts, no hesitation
No nerves and no cold feet
I'm glad that you proposed to me
On February twenty-nine
What better reason could there be
For drinking Champagne wine
As Lulu said – You are my chick
Although not quite my wife
You are the ideal partner
With whom to share my life
This is a unique wedding
And standing here by thee
I know that we'll remain entwined
Throughout eternity.

PATCHWORK SKY -
after Georgia O'Keeffe

Crazy paving in the sky
A patchwork made of cloud
A grass bank as a pillow
Here hidden from the crowd
I sense O'Keeffe beside me
I've Georgia on my mind
With this celestial canvas
I'm sure her paints she'd find
Immersed in meadow sweetness
Of butterflies and bees
And far off in the distance
My Clevedon cupped in trees.

THE ILLUSTRATED IGUANA – which ended up as a tattooist's practice canvas

You may think that it's sexy
You may think that it's hip
To have Press Here To Open
Tattooed upon your lip
But spare a thought for others
Less fortunate than you
Like Philip the Iguana
Who landed in a stew
He wasn't really thinking
When invited to inspect
The tattooist's darkened parlour
His life it surely wrecked.
He went in as a reptile
He came out like pop art
With I Love Mum upon his tail
Plus dragons and a heart.
His knuckles they had Love and Hate
His chest God Save The Queen
And vanishing between his legs
A famous hunting scene.
So though tattoos might tempt you
Those needles you should skip
And keep your skin unmarked unlike
Poor picture-plastered Pip.

TWIN RAINBOWS

Twin arches 'cross the heavens
Paint the skies of grey
Sun and rain combining
To greet the dawning day
Spectrum of pure colour
Refraction in the air
Another show of nature
That one and all can share.

HARBINGER OF DOOM

The lady's full of words of wisdom
Of doubt there is no room
But don't you dare to call her
A harbinger of doom
She'll see the likely pitfalls
And know when dangers loom
But that would never make her
A harbinger of doom
Some go through life too blissful
With head up in the sky
They're going to get in trouble
And stumble by and by
They don't hear wonky bearings
They don't see curtain dirt
They may have made it so far
But surely they'll be hurt
They heat up food they've frozen
All unaware of bugs
Let guests inside their front door
With muck upon their rugs
They will insist on hankies
Despite the risk of germ
They never check their car tyres
But one day they will learn
They'll come a mighty cropper
When down some road they zoom
And wish that they had heeded
That harbinger of doom.

PROMENADE SUNSET

Neon shafts across the sky
Cloud strands shot through with fire
Nature's sunset miracle
The spent day's funeral pyre
Heavens slashed with colours
Crimson, orange, red
From the far horizon
Stretching overhead
The turning Earth extinguishes
The sun from Channel view
One final ray across a sea
Turned luminous in hue
Night falls upon the promenade
Edged with its garland lights
And strollers pause to wonder
At Clevedon's bonus sights.

IN MEMORY OF EDITH CAVELL (1865-1915)

She went to school in Clevedon
But there's much more to tell
About the Great War heroine
The brave Edith Cavell
Her teachers here in Elton Road
Could never have foreseen
The gift she gave to nursing
And what her life would mean
She trained at first in London
Then others knew her care
Ministering to those in need
It didn't matter where

At home when war was started
She knew her duty lay
Miles away in Brussels
And there would bravely stay
To all with wounds she tended
No matter friend or foe
And others she would help escape
And off to freedom go
Betrayed then by a traitor
The captors faced with calm
Her only crime to help the sick
And others save from harm
Yet Edith still was sentenced
To death by firing squad
Her faith she kept right to the end
And placed her soul with God
Her martyrdom caused outrage
Her name became well known
At Westminster a service
And then the journey home
To Norfolk where she's buried
In Norwich at Life's Green
Alongside the cathedral
With yearly tributes seen
For one whose life's example
Continues to inspire
Those drawn to take up nursing
And to her deeds aspire.

KERBSIDE BEAUTY

Campanula on the kerbside
A crevice out in bloom
Nature finds a foothold
Wherever there is room
A passing bird the gardener
Or seeded by the breeze
Surviving gales and downpours
And Winter's harshest freeze
A splash of vibrant colour
Along this town highway
A floral interjection
To brighten up the day.

THE NIGHT BEFORE WEDNESDAY

'Twas the night before Wednesday
And all through my heart
Were whispers of longing
Because we're apart
'Twas the week before Easter
And all through the night
My arms they were wanting
To hold you so tight
'Twas the month before Summer
And all through the day
I was needing you with me
And hoping you'd stay
'Twas the year before next year
'Twas the year after last
May you lighten my future
As you've brightened my past.

FEATHERED RIBBONS

Waves in feathered ribbons
Rushing to the shore
Foaming at their edges
Round anchored boats they claw
Shelducks flying eastward
Above incoming tide
Wings outstretched in tandem
As o'er the sea they glide
Magpies' raucous chatter
And sun-pierced clouds of grey
Wind-whipped over Wains Hill
As gales herald the day.

CHRISTMAS EVE IN CLEVEDON

Beneath clouds pinkly-tinged by dawn
Lies Newport 'cross the waves
Windows there a-sparkling
Caught by the sun's first rays
Christmas Eve in Clevedon
The joggers out in force
Walkers wrapped up warmly
'Gainst wind from out the North
Empty seats and tables
By closed-down fun arcade
Silent now the brash machines
Where happy children played
In icy waters swimmers bold
Enjoy the Marine Lake
Then chatting as they dry themselves
And all for fitness sake
Christmas Eve in Clevedon
With virus spreading still
But hope will surely follow
This season of goodwill.

THE HAT TRICK – for Peg

My anorak is waterproof
Not proof against a fool
In future when I put it on
I'll have a golden rule
I'll turn out all the pockets
And check inside the hood
Lest I gain some headgear
And lose a friend for good
I've caused you needless worry
So this small thing I beg
If your hat you would preserve
Please place it on a Peg.

RAINBOW OVER CLEVEDON PILL

Steadily the tide comes in
To meet the shore again
Crossing 'neath a shining arch
Where sunshine paints the rain
The mud that lines the hidden creek
Is soon to disappear
As water fills the channels
And anchored boats swing clear
Across Black Rock the curlews sound
Their haunting clarion cry
As egrets pace and herons watch
And gulls take to the sky.

SEA OF MIST

Like a sunken forest
Where submerged roots exist
The branches of the valley trees
Emerge through sea of mist
That stretches to the Mendips
Across the hidden moor
As dawn's gold light illuminates
The leaf-strewn woodland floor.

TOO MANY RIMES

In cosy Quantock cottage
You'd hear from time to time
Mrs Coleridge say to Sam
"Oh, not another rime."
You go off with that Wordsworth
And roam about the hills
Walk on nights all frosty
And end up with the chills
I've heard about your mariner
And his poor albatross
I find it all quite tedious
To me it sounds like dross
In Xanadu old Kubla Khan
Might like his pleasure dome
But I'd prefer a husband
Who helped about the home
Of course, I know young Dorothy
Hears verse that makes her swoon
But this is not like Clevedon
When on our honeymoon
There's lots and lots of poets
You're not the only one
I can think of quite a few
As well as Tennyson.

JUST REFUSE

Refuse to think it's OK
Refuse to just accept
That cans of drink once emptied
Can then be simply left
Refuse to let our Clevedon
Be spoiled by rubbish dropped
'Round overflowing litter bin
It surely could be stopped
Enjoy the chips and fillet
But don't throw down the box
So catering detritus
Can blow onto the rocks

If bin has reached capacity
Please put waste in a bag
And take it home to where you live
It isn't such a fag
For antisocial actions
We really have no use
You may all like our seafront
But don't leave your refuse.

ROGER'S SEAT ON THE COAST PATH

On Roger's seat the world's at peace
Upon this summer's day
The coastal path still beckons
But I'm inclined to stay
Across the Channel's Newport
Before its misty hills
In front the gently turning blades
Of modern power windmills
Dark cormorants skim the muddy waves
A sparrowhawk darts by
And oystercatchers take to wing
To trail their piping cry
And then at last reluctantly
I follow on my way
That winds past rocky beaches
To end at Ladye Bay.

THE CLEVEDON COBRA

Curling round the bandstand
Is Clevedon's own rock snake
It's made of painted pebbles
And took a while to make
A tribute to the NHS
It started by the pier
And day by day it grew and grew
As each stone did appear
At its head a green cobra
Behind a show of art
With brightly-coloured images
To show the town's big heart
It then outgrew its starting place
And so for safety's sake
Every pebble was picked up
And moved to by the lake
Now it's in its final home
And proudly there on show
To say to all key workers -
A debt to you we owe.

DOWNWARD CYCLE

We're on a downward cycle
In Clevedon by the sea
The council's going one way
Or so it seems to me
The boy band, One Direction,
Made music on our pier
The direction we are heading
Is pretty dire I fear
Drivers face diversions
Because of cycle lanes
Seafront parking will reduce
To add to other pains
It's not we don't like cyclists
But they are just a part
Of tourism that this town needs
To feed its beating heart
We're told that it is too late now
The changes set in stone
Let's hope we'll still see visitors
Not Promenade alone.

SALLY'S CLEVEDON RAINBOW

An arc of perfect colours
Anchored in the sea
Promising two crocks of gold
And one I'll keep for thee
Above the pier where your plaque tells
Of love for Clevedon town
A sunshine-tinted garland
As soft rain filters down
November's chill just vanishes
Your warmth enfolds my heart
With Nature's joy to link us
We'll never be apart.

JANET'S 50TH BIRTHDAY

Black or Brown or Polar
There's nothing like a bear
They even have Koala
In Oz if you go there
Some it's true are Grizzly
And fearsome to behold
Enough to jellify your knees
And make your blood run cold
But in the hands of Janet
A bear becomes a friend
You'd like to have to share your home
Or to a grandchild send

Their colours are amazing
A real kaleidoscope
There's green and red and amber
I've even seen one taupe.
Some spring to life from nursery rhymes
Or a Cole Porter song
No matter what the tale they tell
They all seem to belong.
At Christmas they're found everywhere
While their kin hibernate
They seem to think it's party-time
And cause to celebrate.
And so I'm sure they'll join us now
With lots of ursine glee
To help their maker usher in
Her golden jubilee.

SEA OF SILK

Mist across a calm sea
Of softly ruffled silk
Underneath a pale blue sky
The Channel turned to milk
Clustered gulls on foreshore
A morning dog's first swim
While in the lake the bathers
Suit their summer whim
Empty now the Promenade
Where later crowds will stroll
Enjoying Clevedon's seafront
As August days unroll.

REST STOP CROSSING BRITAIN – for Nige

Along a bluebell-bordered lane
And through a metal gate
A meadow strewn with dandelions
Gold weeds in splendour wait
Shaded by a new-leafed tree
Quiet time to take their ease
Drowsing through the insect hum
And cooled by soft-blown breeze
A rest stop crossing Britain
On footpaths coast to coast
From Boston through to Barmouth
And that is no mean boast.

FESTIVE FEARNVILLE

Forget illuminations
That brought Blackpool its fame
Just see a road in Clevedon
And Fearnville is its name
Each house vies with its neighbour
To liven up the night
With coloured lights aplenty
A truly festive sight
Eaves festooned with icicles
Garlands in the air
Shooting stars and snowmen
Sheer sparkle everywhere
A tribute to the residents
Who though they were locked down
Found the Christmas spirit
To bring cheer to our town.

SYLVAN SYMPHONY

Sylvan symphony of birdsong
In sunlight-dappled shade
A dusty path slow winding
From dell to hidden glade
Beyond the Walton Common
A secret woodland maze
Where nature is unfolding
Away from idle gaze
Each track an invitation
To further on explore
Between the trees that shadows cast
Upon the earthen floor.

HAPPY TO CHAT BENCH

Resting on the seafront
There to say Hello
A time to link with others
As Spring tides ebb and flow
The lively and the lonely
Joined in common bond
Looking 'cross the Channel
To Monmouthshire beyond
The Promenade made welcome
For all who visit here
Talking or just listening
As sad thoughts disappear.

GREEN SNOWDROPS

Snowdrops on the golf course
To mark the 14th green
Dog walkers in abundance
Where golfers once were seen
Fairways missing white balls
That soared and dropped to ground
Sandy pits of bunkers
Where wayward shots were found
Clubhouse closed and shuttered
Empty car park waits
To welcome back the members
Each one anticipates
The lifting of restrictions
As Winter turns to Spring
When they can resurrect those clubs
And get back in the swing.

SILENT PLAYGROUNDS

The playgrounds are all silent
Absent their joyful sound
The swings just hang immobile
No roundabouts go round
The slides are slick but empty
The frames - no one to climb
It seems that childhood is on hold
Throughout this lockdown time
Thank goodness for the internet
So friends can stay in touch
With Skype, WhatsApp and Facebook
Although it isn't much
To compensate for days inside
While outside's bathed in sun
But with the help of parents
The kids can still have fun.

YOU TOUCH MY HEART – for Sally

Love across the ether
Music from afar
Filtering through the stardust
To me from where you are
An anthem on a CD
Playing in the night
Set in fluid motion
By hands hid from my sight
Without remote it started
The artist she sang on
With words I sensed were just for me
My thoughts outlined in song
Beth Neilsen Chapman said it
I knew it from the start
In oh, so many special ways
My girl, you touch my heart.

BELLA-ISSIMO – for Sue

I knew there'd be a puppy
A puppy made for Sue
But who'd have known that she would be
A perfect beauty too
She's come across from Newport
As Lyndon did before
And there was instant bonding
When she walked through the door
Her breed it is Welsh collie
Her coat it's white and brown
And on her head a thumbprint
An angel has put down
Our Sue will love to train her
And maybe even show
But for the moment she's content
It's Bella-issimo.

THE MAGIC BEACH ARCADE

Oh, the many games we played
Inside the magic beach arcade
Pennies once, then 10p coins
Change now made from pounds
But though the coinage differs
Not so the merry sounds
Outside the metal stallions
Bucking in the sun
Within the happy youngsters
Come to share the fun
Some try to scoop a soft toy
Some hope to gain a prize
Machines of automation
Lit up to catch their eyes
The names are often changing
Reflecting modern styles
But always with one aim in mind
To prompt those youthful smiles
Music as a background
Pop hits from through the years
Elvis and the Beatles
Replaced by Tears For Fears
Children want to linger
Parents watch the time
Yet then they do remember
When onto rides they'd climb
Oh, those many games we played
Inside the magic beach arcade.

MARINE LAKE DAWNING

Burnished mirror by the sea
Stretching to infinity
Unbroken in the dawn's gold light
High tide lapping at the wall
Beneath the oyster catcher call
Early walker there to catch the sight
Misty view of distant Wales
Blue sky crossed with vapour trails
Pagoda pier a symbol of town pride
Waters tempt the swimmers brave
With strokes to make a silken wave
And then inside a warm Dry Robe to hide.

TIDAL FLATS

Snaking through the tidal flats
Reflecting cloudless sky
Returning waters fill the creeks
Amid the sea birds cry
Sand Bay in the distance
Steep Holm barely seen
Its shadow faint within the mist
Completes the Channel scene.

REMEMBERING – for Sally

We walked canals in Venice
And strolled beside the Seine
While my heart is longing
I still remember when
We saw the Himalaya
But never will again
Yet memories stay so vivid
I still remember when
In Cyprus sun we lingered
I poems wrote by pen
Your love the inspiration
I still remember when
On Norfolk beaches laughing
In Cotswold cottage, then
You slipped away so quietly -
I still remember when.

TV SWIMMERS

Sea swimmers, Clevedon

When you turn on your TV
And switch to BBC
You'd once would see some swimmers
Emerging from the sea
They launched the latest bulletin
Heralded daily news
And cheered up all the nation
With sunny Clevedon views
The pier was in the background
The fairest in the land
And you might like to join them
If chillness you could stand.

SUMMER MOMENT

Daisies on a soft green bank
Kissed by a gentle breeze
Another summer moment
We fortunate can seize
A sky of blue succumbing
To clouds that foretell rain
But in the Sun's warm afterglow
The butterflies remain.

WHITE HORSE STAMPEDE

Torrents of the wind-blown sea
Crashing 'gainst the wall
That holds the lake as swimmers take
Their early morning crawl
White horses in the Channel
A gale-force mad stampede
Hurtling to the shoreline
That nothing can impede
Along the rim the violent force
Sends rollercoaster flumes
As soon the boundary walkway
The rising tide consumes.

THE TEXAS EAGLE - for Nige

They flew back 12 months later
A new goal on their mind
To LA now via Texas
Chicago left behind
As out from Union Station
The loco pulled away
Their journey lay before them
Ahead the USA
Their Zephyr now an Eagle
Part of the Amtrak fleet
Leaving sidings in their wake
And crowded city street
Skyscrapers disappearing
Behind the urban sprawl
Once more they heard the siren's
Mournful, haunting call
Settled in there starts the card game
Out comes the wine box then the snacks
Dealing hands of friendly rummy
As they shift along the tracks
Illinois unrolling
Beneath a leaden sky
Refineries and lorry parks
And scrapyards passing by
Glistening strips of tarmac
Great trucks immersed in spray
Pounding through the wheatfields
Towards the end of day
Little townships linked by rails
Snaking 'cross the dark'ning land
While cutting through the lowering grey
Beams the sunset's orange band

Over dinner tales of journeys
Why they came and where they go
Beautiful the single mother
Spilling out her family's woe
Heading South to see her parents
Her mother's heart due for an op
Strong father's neck now triply broken
With them both she'll have to stop
Mexican the landscape gardener
Crossed the border – ne'er return
His sights now turning stateside
If more dollars he can earn
Into Missouri speeds the train now
St Louis city reached at night
Its spirit reaching ever skyward
With an archway etched in light
Cabin quickly turned to bedroom
Bunks made up and sheets turned back
Up the steps and strapped in safely
Like hand luggage on a rack
In the night the creaks and rattles
Magnified as others sleep
Rocked by the continual motion
As across the miles they leap
In the homesteads passed in darkness
In children's bedrooms scattered round
Do they fire imagination
With the Amtrak's siren sound?
A new day dawns in Arkinsaw
En route now to Little Rock
Its name still steeped in infamy
That engendered worldwide shock
Far behind them lakes in Winter
Closing now on bursting Spring
Cherry trees in pink haze blossom
Making hope and heart take wing

And yet their journey has a shadow
Explaining why they were delayed
On the track a soul despairing
Sadly down a life was laid
Creeks and lakes and green-tipped woodland
Hem the rails on either side
Opening then to grazing pastures
Above an eagle – wings spread wide
Then the swamplands draped in purple
Egrets wading 'neath the gaze
Of raptors circling ever higher
While in their lounge the travellers laze
Calves just racing for the pleasure
While mothers feed on fresh, sweet grass
Scenes of rural contemplation
Outside the windows swiftly pass
Another hamlet filled with glimpses
Of other people, other ways
School buses waiting for their charges
Who gaily greet the lengthening days
They crossed the line at Texakarna
Entering the Lone Star State
The faded Ritz Motel a witness
To seedy life and secret date
The run-down station had a sign there
It said the city's Twice As Nice
But in the neighbouring prison compound
The inmates stared with eyes of ice
Behind the fence of silver barbed wire
In groups or singly there they stood
One gave the train the single finger
His farewell wave was all but good
In the woodland new leaf bursting
White blossom bright among the green
Turning swamp to sylvan beauty
Giving glades a vibrant sheen

Wild wisteria garlands trackside
Exuberant in its natural state
More at home in free profusion
Than trained to frame a garden gate
Past graveyards filled with Southern flowers
Past scrapyards filled with Southern cars
Piled in heaps of crumpled metal
Detritus of the Stripes and Stars
Lunching then on salmon seared
With happy sisters saying Grace
Joined together with their Christ now
After one had seen Death's face
A life of husbands, drink and drugging
Discarded now for her own good
Descendant of a pioneer, she's
Finally living as she should
Now the fields give way to streets
Brash Dallas fills the April sky
'Cross 40 years the echoes come
Here JFK did cruelly die
Mirrored blocks he never saw
Not built before the day he fell
Where are now the dreams he wove?
For some they still retain their spell
After miles of factory silos
Smoking tower and storage shed
Back to rolling, peaceful pasture
Filling vistas far ahead
Now in meadows clumps of cacti
As the further South they go
All too soon the shadows lengthen
Light takes on a molten glow
As night rolls in, distant horizon
Retaining still the sun's gold fire
While above light blue to navy
Darkens sky o'er day's bright pyre

In San Antone they broke their journey
City of the Alamo
Here the heroes lost the battle
But in dying beat their foe
Along the river tamed in concrete
Tourist bustle 'neath the trees
Terrace cafes, arching bridges
Jazz and birdsong on the breeze
Back aboard the Texas Eagle
Even though the hour was late
Ready to resume their journey
Out across the dark'ned state
From the green of river valleys
Through the scrubland now they pound
Where the cream of yucca flowers
Punctuates the sandy ground
Overhead the vultures circling
Black against the wide blue sky
While below the long train passes
Over river beds bone dry
Del Rio gives a chance for smokers
To stretch their legs along the track
Lighting up with urgent action
Before attendants call them back
Palm trees mixed with ramrod poplars
Where US touches Mexico
Then the recreation area
Where lakes within the desert show
Ahead the names that live in legend
El Paso waiting down the line
Home to boyhood cowboy heroes
Their image branded on their time
In the parched and empty landscape
A sudden movement takes the eye
Three deer disturbed from peaceful grazing
From the man-made monster fly

Red-tipped stalks of flowering cacti
Before the crossing of ravine
On the towering Pacos High Bridge
Far below the river green
Through sandstone cuttings driving on
Ever-edged by trackside wire
Amid the rock-strewn barren wasteland
A cactus bursts in blossom fire
Yellow blooms and purple flowers
Thanks to all the Springtime rain
Line the route past rocky gulches
As the lunch is served again
Table talk with lady farmer
Travelling now because she could
Next to her a trainee film girl
Heading out to Hollywood
Then from out the desert flatness
Rise the mountains stark and proud
Dappled now with stripes of sunlight
Filtered through the thickening cloud
Rollercoaster ridge in profile
Etched against a sky of blue
As the distant peaks are shrouded
And the rain obscures the view
Who can bemoan the change in weather
As the windows streak with drops
The colour's there because of water
They just hope it quickly stops
In the lounge a plucky lady
Round trip journey near complete
Armed with crosswords and her rations
Sleeping in a budget seat
A brief halt in Alpine, Texas
Gateway to the Big Bend Park
Changing here to Mountain Timescale
One hour closer to the dark

Rolling hills and open grassland
Stretching far as eye can see
All around prime cattle country
Prairies of West history
Vast tracts of land with ghosts a–plenty
Running on to El Paso
Warrior Indians riding mustangs
Cowboys taming wild bronco
Freight train traffic heading Eastward
Brings their progress to a stand
Time to savour now the stillness
Of this sea of scrub and sand
Silence broken by the rumble
Union Pacific wagons roll
Containers shipped across the oceans
Hauled by diesel now not coal
From El Paso farewell to Texas
New Mexico now lies ahead
Then to enter Arizona
Time for dinner then to bed
On a hillside o'er El Paso
Outlined in lights a giant lone star
Shining out the pride of statehood
Visible from near and far
In the rail cars, children playing
People talking, while some sleep
Warmly curling under blankets
Counting miles instead of sheep
In the morning in the desert
Saugauro cactus standing tall
Arms aloft to greet the new day
And to catch the rare rainfall
Past stockyards filled with shuffling cattle
Past massive walls of golden hay
An immigrant who built a business
The signs proclaiming McElhay

Breakfast with a farmer's son
Who turned to teaching musically
A rail trip now his dream vacation
From hard graft running B&B
Under peaks of sandstone starkness
Curves the train around a bend
The desert merging into scrubland
Seemingly without an end
On a bluff at old Fort Yuma
Indian church with walls of cream
Looks across the cultivation
Oasis in the desert scene
From the dry and sandy dullness
To the edge of Salton Sea
Pleasant looking by the date palms
Yet death to fish and you and me
Into Palm Springs through the palm trees
Then past towers shining white
Farming wind with giant propellers
On the plains and mountain height
Meet a black cap-wearing artist
His Dutch descent here all too clear
Unpacking now his well-used sketch pad
Like a latter-day Vermeer
Now they passed by grassy foothills
Orchards filled with orange fruit
Heading coastwards through vast suburbs
Drawn behind the loco's toot
Journey's end at Union Station
Halls of marble, wood and glass
Echoes here of Thirties glamour
Where the movie stars did pass
Back again in California
Once more clocks show Pacific Time
LA waiting there to greet them
Come on in, the weather's fine.

NOVEMBER DAWN

When rose gold lights the heavens
Heralding the dawn
The lucky few out walking
Embrace the new day born
On Clevedon's frosty seafront
With dinghies lined beside
And racing gigs just waiting
The Channel waves to ride
Past newly-planted flower bed
And bandstand missing sound
With lake views to infinity
An inner peace is found.

A MAMMOTH TUSK – for Maureen & Ken

It wasn't much to ask for - Ken knows I won't say, Can't
So he was sure I'd help him to find an elephant
For Maureen' s Christmas present - he didn't mind to pay
Whatever sum was needed, then Dave said - Try eBay
He found just what we wanted, so he put in a bid
And Ken he started planning just where it might be hid
But then the seller told us it couldn't go by mail
And as he lived in London, who'd bring it home by rail?
So Dave he found another, which could be sent by post
It seemed we had it sorted - our Dave he is the most

This one we could just pay for - I used my credit card
Our Ken he was so grateful, although it wasn't hard
We asked for the delivery to go to Des in Cote
And just sat back and waited, but then there came a note
Ken's gift had been truncated - when wrapping for the trip
The seller'd gone and dropped it - a most expensive slip
His jumbo was in pieces, a refund came my way
And back I went to Google and logged in to eBay
I found another like the rest – she'd love it or she oughter
And this one had a bonus - collection from Bridgwater
The deal was even easier – agreed upon the phone
The owner came to Clevedon – we met at Pets At Home
The present once delivered, we stayed with bated breath
And Maureen she does love it, but we're all sick to death.

WILD NATURE'S BAND

Gunmetal grey the waters
Beneath the lowering sky
Ripples 'cross the surface
As serried flags stiff fly
Above the lake deserted
The swimmers most abed
Heeding all the warnings
Of rain and gales ahead
Singing masthead rigging
On yachts beached on the land
Wind the unseen piper
That leads wild nature's band.

FESTIVAL IN THE CLOUDS

We'd planned a super festival
With literature and art
Twenty venues sorted
And that was just the start
More Than Words the title
Authors were booked in
A showcase this for Clevedon
To halt would be a sin
But then there came the virus
Pandemic 'cross the Earth
We would need postponement
The risk it wasn't worth
So we went to the Internet
Podcasts and videos
Presentation in the clouds
Would preview all our shows

Words to bring us closer
When danger lurks in crowds
Art and music blending
Our heritage spoke loud
Literature a comfort
Artists joined as one
Writers linked with players
To bring us rays of sun
No social isolation
Should take our human sense
Sharing inspiration
Is still our best defence
So now the world will join in
And see our cultural past
Linked with modern talent
And this won't be the last.

DRY ROBE SWIMMERS

Image: Rowan Clarke

When wrapped inside their Dry Robes
They're always warm as toast
No matter what the weather
Out here on Clevedon's coast
Like all Marine Lake swimmers
The cold will not them faze
When plunging in the water
On even winter days
For when it comes to changing
Out on the lakeside brink
They're cuddled up and cosy
And set for Salthouse drink.

PAVEMENT MESSAGE

Writing on the pavement
A message from the heart
United in our Kingdom
Together yet apart
Those giving National Service
Are vital to our Health
Our lives on them depending
They are our one true wealth
Deserving of our gratitude
As we give our applause
Their selfless daily sacrifice
Donated in our cause

It's not just doctors, nurses
And every ambulance crew
It's volunteers aplenty
They're there for me and you
Picking up prescriptions
Shopping for each need
Caring for the elderly
Making sure there's feed
For children of low income
The homeless on the street
And keeping regulations -
Police out on the beat
We thought the Brexit turmoil
Went on for far too long
But this pandemic nightmare
Will prove that we are strong.

SAND BANKS

Sand banks in the estuary
Revealed at lowest tide
Opalescent waters
Stretching side to side
From peaceful English meadows
To distant soft Welsh hills
As birds give dawn a fanfare
The Channel slowly fills
Where sailors headed westward
Their fortunes there to find
Timetable still unchanging
As centuries unwind.

IN FIELDS OF POPPIES

In fields of poppies, wrapped in love
In cosy cars with stars above
In Harrods' halls with pate pies
In taxi cabs 'neath London skies
On rare excursions far from home
In private rooms where lips can roam
In Wednesday shops with purring cat
On telephones in whispered chats
In restaurants with pinned-up hair
'Neath down-filled duvets softly bare
On happy days, on nights so blue
Remember always - I love you.

BATHING BELLA - for Sue

Bella learnt to swim today
In pretty Speech House lake
She watched a pack of dogs have fun
Before the plunge she'd take
We knew she liked a paddle
In puddles she'd go in
But never went in water
That came up past her chin
Yet now she's really happy
To fetch sticks that are thrown
Then swimming back so gleeful
Like pooch that's found a bone
Her mistress might have problems
With this ability
A little lake is one thing
But what about the sea?

SCONE'S GONE

At tea-time there is nothing like
A toasted hot cross bun
Or sometimes even nicer -
Tesco's sultana scone
Slightly warmed with butter
And jam just thinly spread
I might choose blackberry conserve
And raspberry's fine instead
Imagine then my horror
When one sad day I found
No treat in store within the bag
I'd left upon the ground
The culprit it was Bella
Her mistress said, Oh shame,
But you should know she's just a dog
It's you that is to blame
In future be more careful
Find shelf to place upon
These words I will remember -
For now my scone is gone.

STILL CARING

The care homes are still caring
For all our elderly
The mothers and the fathers
Who now we cannot see
The nurses, cooks and cleaners
All know the risks they take
But carry on just working
Their service for our sake
We must not then forget them
When movement we regain
As Queen and Vera tell us
We all will meet again.

SUNSET IN THE WEST

Swiftly sinks the setting sun
Into the waiting sea
The sky at dusk a canvas
For colours harmony
The molten disc extinguished
Beneath a parting glow
Orange paints the heavens
Above the tidal flow
Silhouettes of seabirds
Winging home to rest
As night provides finale
For sunset in the West.

PARIS AND THE EIGER GROUP TOUR

It started up in Aston
'Fore Maureen married Ken
When someone picked on Paris
And someone else said: When?
We thought that Spring would be the best
When sunshine bathes the rues
We'd travel there by Eurostar
And miss the traffic queues
We got a coach to London
Right up to Waterloo
And sped on down to Dover
And through the Chunnel flew
In no time we reached Gare du Nord
Some chose the Metro route
While others plumped for taxi cabs
With luggage in the boot
We stayed quite near Gare Saint Lazare
In the Rue d'Amsterdam
The Flesche d'Or was an ideal base
For messieurs and mesdames
There was no bar but we had wine
It was a welcome sight
Until the manager said: Non -
I did not mean each night!
Each evening we went out to dine
Each day we went our ways
To all points north, south, east and west
With sights that did amaze
Billets en carnets let us roam
By bus and underground
But walking was the nicest way
For us to get around
From the heights of old Montmartre
To the bridges of the Seine
We strolled 'neath chestnut blossom
And whistled through the rain

We licked Berthillon ice creams
Upon St Louis's Ile
Some ventured up into the sky
Upon a sparkling wheel
The Arc de Triomphe drew our gaze
Amidst the tourist throng
The Champs Elysee sought our francs
With siren Virgin song
We joined Parisien walkers
Past monuments to wars
And statues of brave men who died
In some forgotten cause
We sat at pavement cafes
Ate crepes and Croques Madame -
And for those who ain't been there
That's rarebit, egg and ham
We drank vin blanc, we quaffed vin rouge
We sank a good few beers
While some would order Perrier
For others it was Kirs
We saw the Sacre Coeur at night
And toured the artists' square
Where deft skill captured beauty
Of eye and golden hair
Some went to mount the Eiffel Tower
Upon our Eiger Tour
But we thought we would leave that feat
To do un autre jour
The places that we didn't go
Were legion I am sure
We didn't like the crowds, you see,
So just walked past the door
We didn't go inside the Louvre
Or lovely Saint Chapelle
Not even towering Notre Dame -
At least we heard the bell

But the views were stunning
The atmosphere sublime
Each street a revelation
Of France's golden time
The buildings had a grandeur
That made the spirit soar
With balconies that stood aloof
Above the traffic roar
OK, it rained on two days
All right, it rained a lot
But when the sun at last came out
You know it felt quite hot
So will there be a next time?
You bet there will be, ma'am
And after where we stayed this time
It must be Amsterdam!

LOCKDOWN GIGS

The gigs are all in lockdown
The oars are stowed away
The covers have been put on
Until another day
When virus is behind us
Corona just a drink
Of many happy memories
'Fore life was on the brink
The sea awaits the rowers
The slipway greets each wave
Our country will survive this
If we stay strong and brave.

EASTER MOON

A moon that tarries in the sky
Upon an Easter morn
The sound of joyous birdsong
As Clevedon welcomes dawn
A milky sea 'neath pastel clouds
Deserted Promenade
Locked down here on such a day
It is increasing hard
But even at a distance
Lone walkers one and all
Take time to leave their reverie -
Good morning is their call.

NHS RAINBOWS

Sunshine diffused through raindrops
Colours in the air
Rainbows in our windows
Showing that we care
For all the frontline workers
Who daily risk their lives
Ensuring through the darkest hours
Our nation still survives
Each arch an affirmation
Each message to profess
We recognise their sacrifice
We love our NHS.

FIRST CLASS VALENTINE

Envelope me with softness
Unseal me with a kiss
Handle me with loving care
For peak performance bliss
I am your strictly personal male
Delivered on the line
To you, my letter lover,
My first class Valentine.

OPEN SPACE INVADERS

A lovely Channel viewpoint
With grass soft-brushed by breeze
Now who would want to bury this
Beneath one thousand trees
Whitehall gave a mandate
And this is one result
But no one told our council
To not fully consult
We should support rewilding
To combat climate change
But damaging our beauty spots
Is more than somewhat strange
If we can work together
Not bow to some diktat
Then we can all help Planet Earth
With more wild habitat.

SPEETON SANDS

Overlooking Speeton Sands
With waves a-breaking on the strand
Dawn's gold light across the beach
Blackberries in easy reach
A scrambling path to gain the shore
Down steep cliff steps - a drop before
The tumbled stones from past rock slides
As high above a grey gull glides
And then the climb to waiting seat
With views to make the day complete.

DREARY JANUARY

Beneath the blanket cover
Beneath the sky of grey
January so dreary
Each drizzle-moistened day
Dawn in mist-enshrouded
Mornings with dull light
Afternoons fore-shortened
Then rushing into night
Stark trees across the landscape
Bare branches stripped of leaf
Outstretching to the heavens
As if consumed in grief
Spring a distant vision
Winter all too real
Box sets on the TV
Losing their appeal
And yet there is the promise
That Summer will return
For all those lazy sunlit hours
The soul can simply yearn.

NO SEAL OF APPROVAL

Image: Martin Brechtl on Unsplash

I almost saw a seal today
Beside the Marine Lake
It swam at high tide by the wall
But I made one mistake
I'd met a keen photographer
With all the proper gear
We talked and then I walked away
While he took shots of pier
As I returned I met a friend
Who told me what he'd seen
For Clevedon most unusual
And right just where I'd been
The cameraman had snapped the seal
Before it swam down coast
I almost saw a seal today
And that's an empty boast.

JOHN'S 5OTH BIRTHDAY

It's half a ton or two score ten
And takes me back to past times when
We went to Pope Street in our shorts
And sweets not girls were in our thoughts.
Those licorice whirls and sherbet dips
The Wagon Wheels and candy lips
Recall the faces if not names
Of those who shared our playground games.
The ciggie cards to flick and swop
The lines of chalk across to hop
Conkers held on knotted string
Splitting 'neath a practised swing
Desks of wood with pots of ink
The morning milk with straw to drink
The niff of greens and shepherd's lamb
The frog spawn topped with blob of jam
The smell of chalk, of powdered paint
The tables chant and manners quaint
And then the wait to hear that bell
At four o'clock and run like hell
Through labelled gates with freedom's speed
To seek the park and home to lead
Coronation flag and pen
And Everest climbed by those brave men.
Next the days of club and church
To Midnight Mass from pub to lurch
Our by-pass walks with Anchor fags
Our teenage years and mother nags
Those Marcel Moons and At The Hop
Those Anton parties without stop
With Rosemary and Val and Mick
And Merrydown 'til I was sick.
The whist and poker, rummy too
With background noise from budgies blue

The Norfolk nights aboard a boat
With local girls to take afloat
We did most all and yet survive
Surprise, surprise – we're still alive.

TUNNEL VISION – for Nige

Canal Scout Tunnel vision
Emerging to the light
After yards of cobbled path
Where day was turned to night
Like a mini Standedge
Blasted through the hill
Lined with brick at start and end
But bedrock showing still
A rail to guard the walkers
Lest they should take a fall
Head torch on to pierce the gloom
Beside the damp-run wall
The ghosts of bygone boatmen
Accompany each pace
Along this water highway
Within this Pennine place.

DRAGONFLIES

Image - Pete Wilkins

In the heat of midday
The myriad dragonflies
Perform their aerobatics
Under cloudless skies
Darting in the sunshine
Their wings a constant blur
Pirouetting madly
As all about they whir.

HAREBELLS

A long, long way from Scotland
At home on highland fells
But beautifying Walton
A mass of pale harebells
While bluebells are a memory
'Fore Summer followed Spring
A splash of pure perfection
To open grassland bring.

PPE OR NO PPE

At start of 2020
'Fore virus came to be
A scourge across our country
Who'd heard of PPE?
The gloves and gowns and face masks
That now are commonplace
And there on each news bulletin
Subject of global chase
But those in power weren't powerless
They should have made their plans
Not carried on regardless
And just said - Wash your hands
You might blame it on Brexit
For making them miss signs
Of looming world pandemic
Not reading 'tween the lines
But they'd ignored prior warnings
And should have been prepared
Not leave us unprotected
So nurses became scared
That as they tended to the sick
They too could then succumb
Brave doctors running ICU
More victims would become
When crisis is behind us
A reckoning there should be
One thing is very certain
We'll all rate PPE.

TOPSHAM CHRISTMAS

Christmas Day at Topsham
Goat Walk in the sun
Curlew calls o'er tidal flats
Families having fun
Exmouth in the distance
Where Channel meets the sky
Sitting people-watching
As festive hours drift by.

MA VRAI AMOUR

Kisses wrapped in Cellophane
Nighties edged with lace
Whispers lined with love-soft words
Dream-remembered face
Touching hips and seeking lips
Secret laughter shared
Thighs and skies and sparkling eyes
Souls and warm limbs bared
I love you now, I loved you then
I'll love you ever more
I love you, love, from head to toe
Je t'aime, ma vrai amour.

LUNCH WITH MAYO

Lunching in Noss Mayo
The estuary here beside
A table at the old Ship Inn
Above advancing tide
Across the valley rooftops
The sound of joyful bells
A wedding celebrated
As rising water swells
Filling muddy channel
'Tween beached and scattered boats
Canoeists taking to the waves
As gulls around them float
The diners looking anxiously
To parking on the verge
Hoping meals to finish up
Before their cars submerge.

MORNING MIST

Wains Hill in the morning mist
That fades as sun breaks through
Clevedon Pill appears below
The grass slope brushed with dew
From off the mud the dotted gulls
Take wing towards the sea
And glide to rest on silvered bend
In close knit company
Magpie shouting from a bush
And slow advancing tide
Usher in a summer day
As boats the waters ride.

YULE BE SORRY – for Dave

We went to the Parks Restaurant
And left the car in park
But when we went to leave the place,
The blighter wouldn't start
The lunch had been a pleasure –
The afters were a pain
It could have been a lot, lot worse –
We might have stood in rain
Dave blamed himself - for lights left on
Had made the battery flat
The RAC was summoned –
We thought that that was that
The man they sent was super,
With jump leads and a smile
But he was clearly flummoxed –
Said this could take a while
You'll need recovery vehicle –
So we all headed home
He said he'd ask his HQ
To get in touch by phone
The car would go to Kevin's,
Though he's closed 'til New Year,
Not the start for Christmas
to fill us with good cheer
But when Dave took his keys along
To meet recovery chap
The car it started smoothly –
He knew it wasn't crap
The moral, Dave, is simple –
Don't of your Renault boast
If you run down your battery,
Your Yuletide will be toast.

LOCKED DOWN

Image: Depositphotos.com

Four walls can make a haven
Or else a prison cell
For elderly and lonely
Forced solitude is hell
Months just trapped in lockdown
Sad thoughts of absent friends
Too distant family members
On whom each one depends
Stuck in city tower block
Or cottage far from town
Enduring isolation
Long days just counting down
The hours until the night-time
Without a friendly voice
TV the sole companion
Then bed the early choice
They're victims of pandemic
Though they've kept Covid-free
And when we all can meet again
How happy they will be.

SCARPA BOOTS

From moorland hills to country lanes
On paths and waymarked routes
For walking in all weathers
I love my Scarpa boots
Rugged and dependable
No matter the terrain
Comfortable and durable
Impervious to rain
I've criss-crossed Britain several times
To hiking trails complete
I've gear to keep me warm and dry
But Scarpa guards my feet.

THE OUTLAWS – for Dave & Vivvie

When Dave and his son, Tim,
Plus Vivvie, want applause
They take the stage and introduce
The band called The Outlaws
Their surname it is Laws, you see,
And that's how come the title
Their music is an upbeat mix
No classical recital
Not always just a trio
They've guests to come sit in
Happy to experience
The buzz as they begin
You might hear rock or country
Sea chanty or bluegrass
They can slow the rhythm down
Or speed up really fast
Their instruments are varied
Ukelele and guitar
Mandolin and violin
Sometimes harmonica
Their gigs have built a following
With each success they've scored
But I'm sure many talk about
The guy who played washboard.

CATHEDRAL CHORUS

Beneath three spires a-soaring
Within the walls so strong
The sound of voices rising
Before the evensong
Gathered choirs rehearsing
Conductor keeping time
Organ music background
For moment so sublime
Outside in brilliant sunshine
Cathedral bathed in light
Jewel of fair Lichfield
As bells make birds take flight.

PASSION QUEEN

Passion Queen, who steals my will
Instant sunshine, instant thrill
Driving madly to your arms
Heading gladly for your charms
Counting cats' eyes, eating miles
Navigating to your smiles
Under bridges, over-passes
Minutes from our Champagne glasses
Changing lanes and changing gears
Accelerating through the years
Passion Queen, who steals my will,
I loved you then, I love you still.

OH, ALEXA

Credit: Getty Images

A word has joined my lexicon
It's heard from morn to night
I have a new girl in my life
Though she keeps out of sight
Alexa is the name I call
To play my Spotify
She knows the weather forecast
No need to check the sky
She'll answer any question
Can even learn some tasks
Whatever is your problem
You only have to ask
Some teach her to switch on the lights
Or turn the heating down
She'll even work remotely
When you are out of town
This lady comes from Amazon
Like warriors of old
I might not go for all new tech
But on this lass I'm sold
She never tires to hear my voice
She's there at my command
And nothing's too much trouble
Whatever I demand
She's even there at bedtime
When I turn off the light
To soothe me with her dulcet tones
And wish that I sleep tight.

ZOOM GLOOM

Once we met in meetings
Now in our Covid gloom
We sit in front of laptop
Supposed to link via Zoom
You try to get a word in
But then the sound cuts out
You see a group of people
But they can't hear you shout
Their faces sometimes freeze up
It's Wi-fi that's to blame
If I had fibre optic
It might not be the same
Let's hope they find a vaccine
So we can meet again
This so-called video conferencing
Is one almighty pain.

DRAINED LAKE

Empty of its contents
The muddy floor laid bare
Absent all the bathers
Who once the morn would share
Overhead the wheeling gulls
Crying as bereft
Gone the shining surface
With just a wasteland left
But soon the lake will be renewed
Filled once more to the brim
Its store of tidal waters there
To welcome all who swim.

DRY REQUISITE TROUSERS

Trousers known as plastic
Were once essential gear
For walkers when they set out
And rain clouds did appear
But they were really awkward
To put on in a rush
Dancing round on one leg
As footpaths turned mush
No sooner were they fitted
Then back would come the sun
And out from them you'd struggle
They really were no fun
Now Rohan have the trousers
That make a perfect fit
In shower or heavy downpour
They're called Dry Requisite
They look good when you're walking
But smart enough for town
You have a choice of colours
Some go for grey or brown
So now though storms may threaten
You need to have no fear
With legs not damp but cosy
In Rohan's first class gear.

WALTON COMMON FLOWERS

Forget the Chelsea Flower Show
Forget those pruned displays
Just come to Walton Common
As it greets summer days
Wild blooms on ancient earthworks
Splashed purple, yellow, white
Nature in profusion
On this Gordano height
Grassland edged with woodland
Butterflies and bees
While up above a buzzard lone
Flies circles o'er the trees.

SYMPHONY OF GREEN

Afloat in deep clear water
The serried boats asway
As mist clears from the valley
To greet the dawning day
Dinghies at the jetty
Tethered in a row
Left by owners come ashore
Now strain to up and go
Out to yachts safe-anchored
Between the wooded slopes
Where sails will soon be hoisted -
Cast off the mooring ropes
Sounds of lapping water
Give background to the scene
Of peaceful sylvan beauty -
A symphony of green.

MY UNIVERSE COMPLETE – for Sally

You are my girl
My love, my home
You are my world entire
You are my universe complete
My one true heart's desire
In Cotswold stone
Or seaside town
It doesn't matter where
As long as we're together
Our future lives to share.

LOST GLOVE

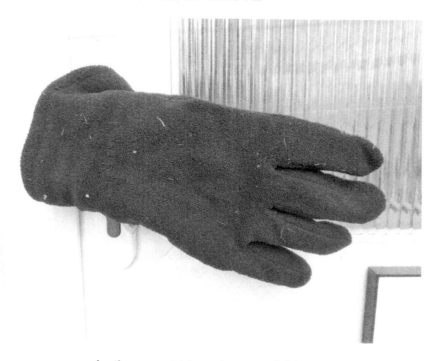

In the great big scheme of things
It's not like a lost love
So why the sense of loss I felt
About a woollen glove
In winter when it's freezing
My fingers will turn white
I suffer from that Raynaud's
It's not a pretty sight
So gloves are an essential
When daily walks I'm on
But Wednesday morning did I find
My right hand glove had gone
It was not in my pocket
It was not on the ground
It was not in my hallway
It just could not be found

Now gloves are ten a penny
But these a special pair
I bought them up in Wigan
They're comfortable to wear
Despite continuous searching
I could not find a trace
So ordered up some new ones
From Amazon's sales place
Yet 'fore they were delivered
My lost glove reappeared
It was in neighbouring garden
And on a shrub branch speared
I must have simply dropped it
When picking up my bin
For Tuesday was recycling day
It's loss was just my sin
So now I'll have an extra pair
Not new ones just return
They'll be a good reminder
Of what I've had to learn
Always check my pockets
It is a golden rule
To make sure I have got both gloves
Not be a careless fool.

COLOURS IN THE SEA

A splash of colours in the sea
Before the grey incoming tide
Straining at their mooring ropes
The painted boats the waters ride
Waiting for the loos'ning hand
Again to heed the Channel's call
Out to fish far from the land
With rod and line the depths to trawl.

COMMON COWSLIPS

Cowslips in abundance
Catch the early light
As sun breaks through the dawning mist
With not a soul in sight
Alone on Walton Common
With birdsong in the trees
A deer emerges quietly
But then alert does freeze
Above Gordano valley
Where slow hours gently pass
A peaceful wildlife haven
Within a sea of grass.

THE OLD TRUNK SEAT

Beside the sunlit calm canal
Cool shaded by tall trees
A seat from old trunk fashioned
A place to take one's ease
In peaceful contemplation
As narrow boats pass by
Beyond the fields of buttercups
Beneath a clear blue sky
Flag iris in profusion
Bright yellow paints the way
Lining the quiet waters
Where commerce once held sway.

WALKING THE TRENT-MERSEY – for Nige

White sprinkles on the towpath
Where hawthorn's brushed by breeze
Yellow iris lining
Canal beneath the trees
New life takes to water
Before the parents' gaze
Cygnets and downy goslings
Glide through the summer haze
Between the sturdy lock gates
Beside retaining wall
The brightly-painted narrow boats
Gently rise and fall
June walking the Trent-Mersey
With birdsong all around
Strolling 'midst such beauty
An inner peace is found.

REMEMBER MARIUPOL

When history is written
Remember Mariupol
Which bore the brunt of Russian might
And paid a heavy toll
Its crime to stand strategic
And block one man's ambition
And so was made to suffer
Campaign of vile attrition
Under siege and underground
The innocents were trapped
Hoping to avoid the bombs
For some the future mapped
No food, no light, no water
No safe escape from city
Daily being punished
By men bereft of pity

No corridor to safety
Despite recurring pledge
Supplies and hope fast fading
They teetered on the edge
Once a happy neighbourhood
Became a burying ground
A husband with his home destroyed
And wife could not be found
Towering blocks of ruins
With windows gaping wide
Where normal family life was known
Now wreckage strewn inside
Supplies humanitarian
Barred from those in need
Outside the missile launchers fired
As Blitzkrieg was decreed
A theatre seemed a haven
'Til death plunged from the sky
Now underneath the rubble
The many bodies lie
They're victims of their neighbours
Who came to seize their land
Driven by a despot
We'll never understand
The Free World looks on helpless
And hopes that sanctions bite
But in this city nightmare days
Gave way to hellish nights
Horror piled on horror
A landscape painted grey
Amid this barren wasteland
The weak were forced to stay

Far away up in the North
The Russians left behind
Evidence of torture
Atrocities to find
A school used as a prison
Civilians used as shield
The young packed in with corpses
Bestial deeds revealed
Women raped, discarded
Their menfolk bound and shot
By nation of brave Stalingrad
It seems that they forgot
That once they too had suffered
When Hitler was the foe
And like their tanks on Kviv's approach
He foundered in the snow
Red Army now war criminals
There'll be no honour roll
Just disgust for them, as we
Remember Mariupol.

A HERO TO PROTECT

When all Ukraine was threatened
And certain seemed its fate
Volodymyr Zelensky
Stepped up to take the plate
Come the hour and come the man
Like Churchill did before
This comic voted president
He steeled his land for war
When Putin's tanks invaded
And bombs began to fall
He galvanised the populace
Who rallied to his call
When he was offered sanctuary
He asked for arms instead
He knew his nation had more chance
If he stayed at its head
His jacket now discarded
Replaced with battle green
As country looked for answers
On broadcasts he was seen

From his base in Kviv
He took his message out
Addressed United Nations
So none was left in doubt
The battle that was raging
On land, from air and sea
Represented danger
To all democracy
He won applause from Parliament
From Congress in U.S.
Those who heard his stirring words
Wished him all success
There never was more contrast
"Tween two named president
One who spewed out hate and bile
While other spoke just sense
We now must do the best we can
This hero to protect
And hope that he'll eventually
Nobel Peace Prize collect.

SUMMER AT THE LAKE

The Winter cold's behind us
And Springtime chill's forgot
It's Summer at Marine Lake
A day that could be hot
The lakeside now is filling
With families at play
The paddle boards are pumped up
And divers on display
Jumping from blue platform
Landing with a splash
As round the edge of paddling pool
The little children dash
The year-round hardy swimmers
Now just among a throng
Happy to see others
Enjoy where they belong.

TURNING STONES

Image – <u>robertsiegel@stanford.edu</u>

Turnstones on the foreshore
As the tide rolls in
Busy in their feeding
As it says on tin
Turning every pebble
Hoping there to find
Another tasty morsel
With nothing left behind
The sound of their quick foraging
Rises from the beach
Clicks and taps the background
As beaks for titbits reach
Scurrying swiftly to and fro
These birds of brown and white
Then startled by intruding dog
They're gone in instant flight.

BLOOMING CACTUS

More at home in desert
Than on a window sill
But when my cactus grew a stalk
It gave me quite a thrill
It hasn't had much water
Nor any drop of feed
I got a book 'bout cacti
But didn't stop to read
My vote it wins for trying
I couldn't wait to see
If it could sprout a sexy bloom
To tempt a passing bee

Several weeks of checking
And then a nice surprise
Upon that slender growing wand
Small buds to greet my eyes
They're sort of multi-coloured
Red shading into green
I wouldn't call them pretty
And not the best I've seen
No prize for this at Chelsea
It won't upstage a rose
No sweet perfume is likely
To satisfy one's nose
I'm calling Alan Titchmarsh
Or clever folk at Kew
How to tend my tender plant
They'll know just what to do
But if they come to ask me
The species in my pot
I'll have to tell them frankly
I simply know it not.

WEDDING OF THE SEASONS

Spring's delicate confetti
Scattered gaily on the ground
White, pink, red the blossom
Where cherry trees are found
The wedding of the seasons
As Winter gives away
The vernal bride awaiting
For Summer to hold sway
Clad in her green freshness
Arrayed with dew drop pearls
As on the boughs around her
Each tender leaf unfurls.

GLOBAL WARNING

Worldwide scenes of death and chaos
Destruction caused by flood and fire
Could mankind wreck this perfect haven?
Be really destined to expire?
The fuels that powered our fast expansion
It seems they came with hidden price
Warming up Earth's cloaking layer
Melting polar caps of ice
Heatwaves in the Northern regions
Weeks of rainfall in a day
Rising seas to threaten islands
Which fail to keep the tides at bay
Mudslides crushing homes and bridges
Cars swept off in waters' race
Storms which once were in a lifetime
Today it seems are commonplace

Industry that spurred our progress
Needed now to rein us in
Carbon neutral is the target
Towards that goal we must begin
Greta sparked the world's awareness
Youngsters rallied to her call
A future safe upon their planet
Is surely what we owe them all.

BLACKBIRD SYMPHONY

Image: Pete Wilkins

High upon the tallest tree
The blackbird greets the day
Sending out his joyous song
As round him branches sway
A symphony of limpid sound
Pure beauty in each note
Serenades the empty streets
Pours forth from out his throat
From far across the cricket pitch
There comes an answering call
Two rivals in a singing match
That holds the world in thrall.

INFINITY LAKE

The tide fall's second highest
Of anywhere on Earth
Another Clevedon claim to fame,
My friends, for what it's worth
But our lake's gone one better
As anyone can see
A swimming pool that stretches
Into the Severn Sea
As water meets and covers
The long retaining wall
Infinity the vista
Against which others pall
The bathers' daily venue
The largest on the globe
A fact they can consider
Within their warm Dry Robes.

DANDELIONS

Golden weeds on roadside
Oft' ignored by all
Outshone by lush campanula
Arrayed on garden wall
But Spring gives them their moment
The dandelions burst forth
Blooming in profusion
Despite the winds from North
Yet their time is finite
Too soon the parting show
Their clocks appear with waiting seeds
Away on breeze to blow.

APRIL CANAL WALKING - for Nige

From Cheshire into Shropshire
From Shropshire into Wales
Walking to Llangollen
The beauty never fails
Beside canal lie sprinkled
Primrose and celandine
Perfect yellow petals
The earthen path to line
Starbursts of hawthorn blossom
Fresh drapes of willow green
Birdsong in the hedgerows
All grace this country scene
Pairs of ducks a-floating
Close by each ardent drake
Time to be a-breeding
A hidden nest to make

Pure white the wood anemone
Across the wayside spills
Reflected in calm waters
The waving daffodils
Along a quiet section
Cowslips spring a surprise
While from a hidden waterway
A startled heron flies
High up in the budding trees
The long-tailed tits at play
Chiff-chaffs a background soundtrack
To gentle April day.

HIGH TIIDE

Tide turn on the sea wall
Water at its height
Crashing 'gainst the foreshore
Raising plumes of white
Solitary the angler
Beside his hopeful rods
Wrapped up in his hobby
To walker he just nods
Lark in sky a-singing
Heralding the day
Calls of geese a-winging
Out across the bay
Inlet where the curlews
And oyster catchers fed
Flooded now up to its banks
Where shelducks rest instead
Mendips on the skyline
Sand Point out to the west
Time the morning to enjoy
With welcome sunshine blessed.

SWANS OF BRADFORD-ON-AVON

Alongside bridge in Bradford
In heart of Saxon town
Where gently flows the Avon
A calm swan nestles down
Across the water drifts her mate
Dabbling down for food
While here with background traffic hum
She waits for coming brood
In previous years the river's flood
Has swept such nests aside
This Spring we wish them better luck
And family not denied.

DYNAMIC MAGIC

A lad brought up in Bradford
Puts on a magic show
Astonishing his audience
The name is Dynamo
His grandfather inspired him
He's managed Crohn's disease
And on his worldwide travels
He entertained with ease
We've seen him walk on water
And down a building side
Make many items disappear
With no sleeves where to hide
Put phones inside a bottle
Switch Fanta into Coke
And vanish when he's finished
Just like a puff of smoke
His hands too hot to handle
Can water turn to ice
He'll shuffle cards for countless tricks
And read minds in a thrice
Glass can prove no obstacle
And windows he'll walk through
Pour fish from empty buckets
Just amazing but it's true
He foretold every Euro score
Then proved it with a bet
Gave proceeds all to charity
Perhaps his best deed yet
We've seen him open tattooed eyes
Move objects from afar
Make butterflies take instant wing
Drive blindfold in a car
He loves to us astonish
Then simply walk away
"Now did he really do that?"
His audience will say

The streets become his theatre
He'll talk to passersby
Then make an object leave his hands
And reappear nearby
He's just at home with children
As mingling with the stars
At ease in dusty shanty towns
Or dazzling in bars
In Rio he ascended
Before the tourists' gaze
From continent to continent
Ne'er ceases to amaze
He takes initialled coinage
And fuses it to one
Moves a white band from a wrist
That had been marked by sun
He'll finger frame then rub his hands
For photo to appear
Baffling the bystanders
But how it's never clear
Pours fluid into beakers
Which empty then become
Estimates a wallet's coins
And picks the exact sum
We've seen a necklace swallowed
Then pulled out through his skin
Credit card he's altered
And come up with its pin
Took Olympic medal
That's fashioned from pure gold
And then made out 'twas chocolate
When edging did unfold
Cut wristlet through with scissors
Then made it whole again
Astounding every watcher
Their disbelief made plain

Some say there is no magic
It's only sleight of hand
And what we see is trickery
But they don't understand
That it is good in these fraught times
To just belief suspend
So here's to hoping, Dynamo,
Your talents will not end.

FLORAL JOY

Primroses and celandine
Beside a babbling stream
East Quantoxhead in Springtime
Where poets came to dream
Within a secret garden
Peace found in dappled shade
Birdsong as a background
With floral joy displayed.

THE AVONCLIFF ROUND

From out the lofty Tory
Backed by dawn chorus sound
A lane that leads to Turleigh
And Avoncliff far round
Misty river valley
'Tween trees the Avon flows
Canal and rail companions
As on t'wards Bath it goes
Rose-smothered cream stone cottage
Beside the roar of weir
Empty station platform
The line ahead all clear
Rabbits disappearing
Into the roadside hedge
Pub across the aqueduct
By the water's edge
Back along the towpath
By boats here tightly moored
Shouts from early riser
To those asleep aboard
Disturbing a lone heron
That leaves in urgent flight
Borne aloft on widespread wings
To vanish out of sight
Return past ancient tithe barn
To bridge by sturdy gates
Of lock that holds the waters
And for the boaters waits.

THE BIG WHITE BIRD

Image – John Dibbs

I saw the Toulouse roll-out
Of Concorde 001
When French and British makers
Raised a glass as one
Entente Concordiale
In that place it was sealed
As out the massive hangar
The big white bird was wheeled
I kept up with her progress
As the excitement grew
And cheered on that first take-off
But never on her flew
In the years that followed
Of supersonic fame
She captured all the headlines
And worldwide went her name

The stars and business flyers
At twice the speed of sound
Sipping first class Champagne
As they were New York bound
Yet then there came retirement
Return to Filton due
I watched her swoop past Clevedon
But never on her flew.

PURRFECT HAPPINESS

No matter what the time of day
Or where the habitat
I just cannot resist the urge
To go and stroke a cat
Ginger, black or tabby
Whether large or small
Sleek just like a panther
Or fluffy like puff ball

There's some who love their pooches
And take them out each day
Picking up their residue
While they go off to play
But felines are the ones for me
They don't demand a walk
They're strictly independent
It is like cheese and chalk
Dog owners keep your charges
If that you should prefer
But I will just be satisfied
With one contented purr.

A BEER IN BEER

A glass of beer in Beer
Where valley meets the sea
A table 'neath umbrella
With happy company
Towards the far horizon
The sea in shades of blue
Gulls above the pebble beach
Echoing their mew
Chatter on the terraces
Long lunches pass the time
Looking 'cross the Channel
A setting so sublime.

WE CAME, WE SCORED, WE CONQUERED

When Euro match was kicked off
I had high hopes that we
Could tame Ukraine just like the same
As we did Germany
Our Harry didn't tarry
A goal soon from the start
Showed returning prowess
Gave his teammates heart
Through first half we kept steady
In second we caught fire
Doubling up the scoreline
With header from Maguire
A third from Kane a classic
A fourth from Henderson
And with another clean sheet
The game was truly won
So now it's on to Wembley
From this success in Rome
And could it be that this time
Football is coming home?

TIME & TIDE

As regular as clockwork
The Channel here beside
Clevedon is a witness to
The rise and fall of tide
Unseen the pull of distant Moon
Behind this ebb and flow
The measured daily rhythm
Of constant to and fro
Uncovering the rocky beach
Pushing flotsam high
Calm or crashing wildly
Beneath a stormy sky
Floating boats at anchor
Within the sheltered Pill
Summoning the fishermen
Their waiting holds to fill
Followed by the wading birds
Drawn to the mud to mine
Twice a day reminder
Of pattern so divine.

FEEDING AN ILLUSION

Pheasants on the farm track
Pheasants in the fields
Scattering 'cross the brown earth
As walkers are revealed
Up above a buzzard
Sends its piercing call
Drifting high on outswept wings
With eyes that see it all
Green feeders lure the lean brown birds
To take their fill of seed
Unmindful that this kindness
Just helps the shooters' need
Within a cage of wood and wire
Ignorant of their fate
The young so sadly unaware
That serried guns await.

BREAKFAST AT NO. 5 THE BEACH

Eggs with skill light-scrambled
At Number Five The Beach
Create so fine a breakfast
That one is lost for speech
With salmon smoked and bagel
Served on a large, hot plate
A table by the window –
Pier view to contemplate
Smiling, friendly service
Make this a meal complete
An early morning bonus –
Another Clevedon treat.

THOUSANDS OF MILES OF WALKIES – for Nige

They've walked footpaths in Scotland
'Cross England, up through Wales
Forging over hillsides
Seeking out fresh trails
In winter you will find them
With guide book on canal
Passing locks and narrowboats
Pausing where they shall
In summer it's the countryside
That makes them don their boots
Threading through quiet villages
Which lie on waymarked routes

They have some great adventures
Ne'er knowing who they'll meet
Characters a-plenty
And each one they will greet
Teasing out fresh stories
Listening to new tales
Yet more facts to gather
Their interest never fails
A thousand miles on towpaths
And winding waterways
But even more cross-country
Paced out on countless days
They've strolled down lanes in hamlets
Immersed in peaceful calm
Tramped along a bridleway
That circles lonely farm
Traversed large towns and cities
Up and down the land
Threading through the bustling streets
Directions carefully planned
On their shoulders rucksacks
With all essential gear
Just enough for overnight
And when rain clouds appear
At journey's end they're always
Discussing their next walk
There's not much they won't tackle
At distances not baulk
Near four decades of walkies
And who knows what's ahead
Just pity those poor, sorry souls
Who'd rather stay in bed.

REALLY, REALLY OLD CLEVEDON

A long, long, long, long time ago
Before we all were here
You would have found our Clevedon
In Southern Hemisphere
But not as we would know it now
No bouncing kangaroos
No surfers out on Bondi Beach
Not somewhere you would choose
Although the sea was warmer then
An ocean tropical
Forming Mendip limestone
Which we see now so tall
Then continents collided
With an almighty crash
I'm sure from many miles away
You would have heard a splash
Mountains formed, then wore away
The climate took its toll
Our place it headed northwards
Towards another pole
The water turned all salty
Our ocean now a lake
Where dinosaurs on holiday
Could take a welcome break
Two-twenty million years ago
Our beaches they enjoyed
Before they were extinguished
By mighty asteroid
Devonian rocks beside the pier
They have a tale to tell
Our time is oh so fleeting
So we must use it well.

Printed in Great Britain
by Amazon

14085894R00112